EXTREME SPORTS
Maria Koran
EYEDISCOVER

Go to www.openlightbox.com and enter this book's unique code.

BOOK CODE

AVA43752

EYEDISCOVER brings you optic readalongs that support active learning.

Published by Lightbox Learning Inc.
276 5th Avenue, Suite 704 #917
New York, NY 10001
Website: www.openlightbox.com

Library of Congress Control Number: 2022935920

ISBN 978-1-7911-4872-0 (hardcover)
ISBN 978-1-7911-4874-4 (multi-user eBook)

Printed in Guangzhou, China
1 2 3 4 5 6 7 8 9 0 26 25 24 23 22

042022
102121

Project Coordinator: John Willis
Designer: Ana María Vidal

Photo Credits
Every reasonable effort has been made to trace ownership and to obtain permission to reprint copyright material. The publisher would be pleased to have any errors or omissions brought to its attention so that they may be corrected in subsequent printings. The publisher acknowledges Alamy, Getty Images, and Shutterstock as its primary image suppliers for this title.

EYEDISCOVER provides enriched content, optimized for tablet use, that supplements and complements this book. EYEDISCOVER books strive to create inspired learning and engage young minds in a total learning experience.

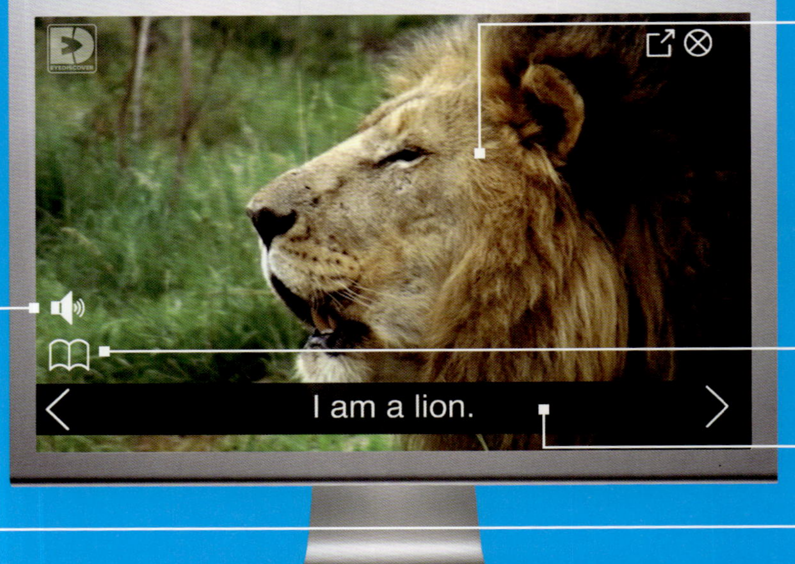

Watch
Video content brings each page to life.

Browse
Thumbnails make navigation simple.

Read
Follow along with text on the screen.

Listen
Hear each page read aloud.

Your EYEDISCOVER Optic Readalongs come alive with...

Audio
Listen to the entire book read aloud.

Video
High resolution videos turn each spread into an optic readalong.

OPTIMIZED FOR
- TABLETS
- WHITEBOARDS
- COMPUTERS
- AND MUCH MORE!

This title is part of our EyeDiscover digital subscription

1-Year EyeDiscover Subscription
ISBN 978-1-4896-8346-5

Access all EyeDiscover titles with our digital subscription.
Sign up for a FREE trial at **www.openlightbox.com/trial**

EXTREME SPORTS

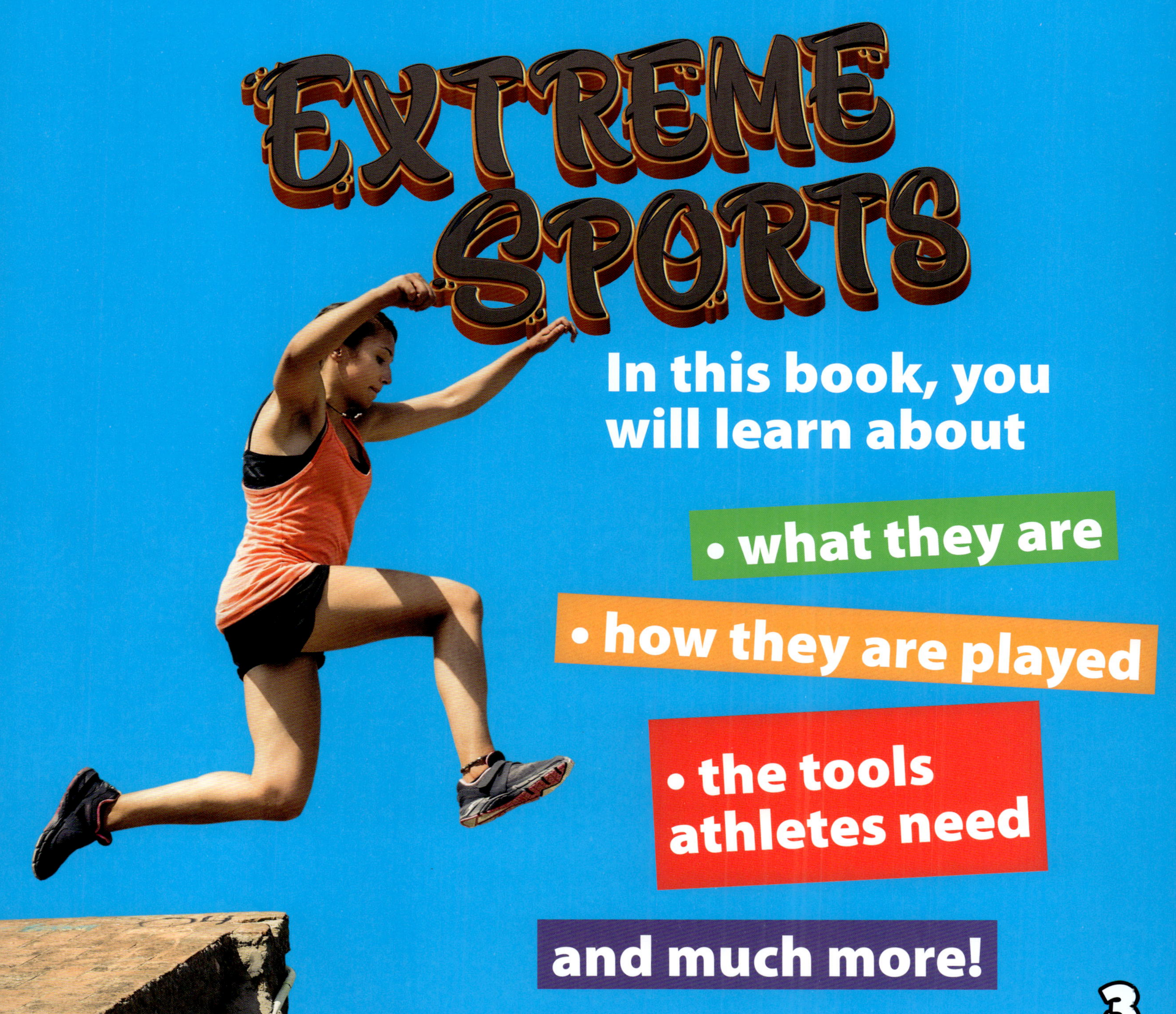

In this book, you will learn about

- what they are
- how they are played
- the tools athletes need

and much more!

Extreme sports are very exciting. Athletes often need to use special tools for these sports.

Bungee jumpers jump from high places. A cord stops them from hitting the ground. They bounce instead.

Skydivers jump from airplanes. They use parachutes to slow their fall and land safely.

BASE jumping is one of the most dangerous extreme sports. BASE jumpers use parachutes to jump from high places.

Street luge riders lay down on wheeled boards called sleds. They race downhill at high speeds.

Red Bull
excite
30
gravitysports

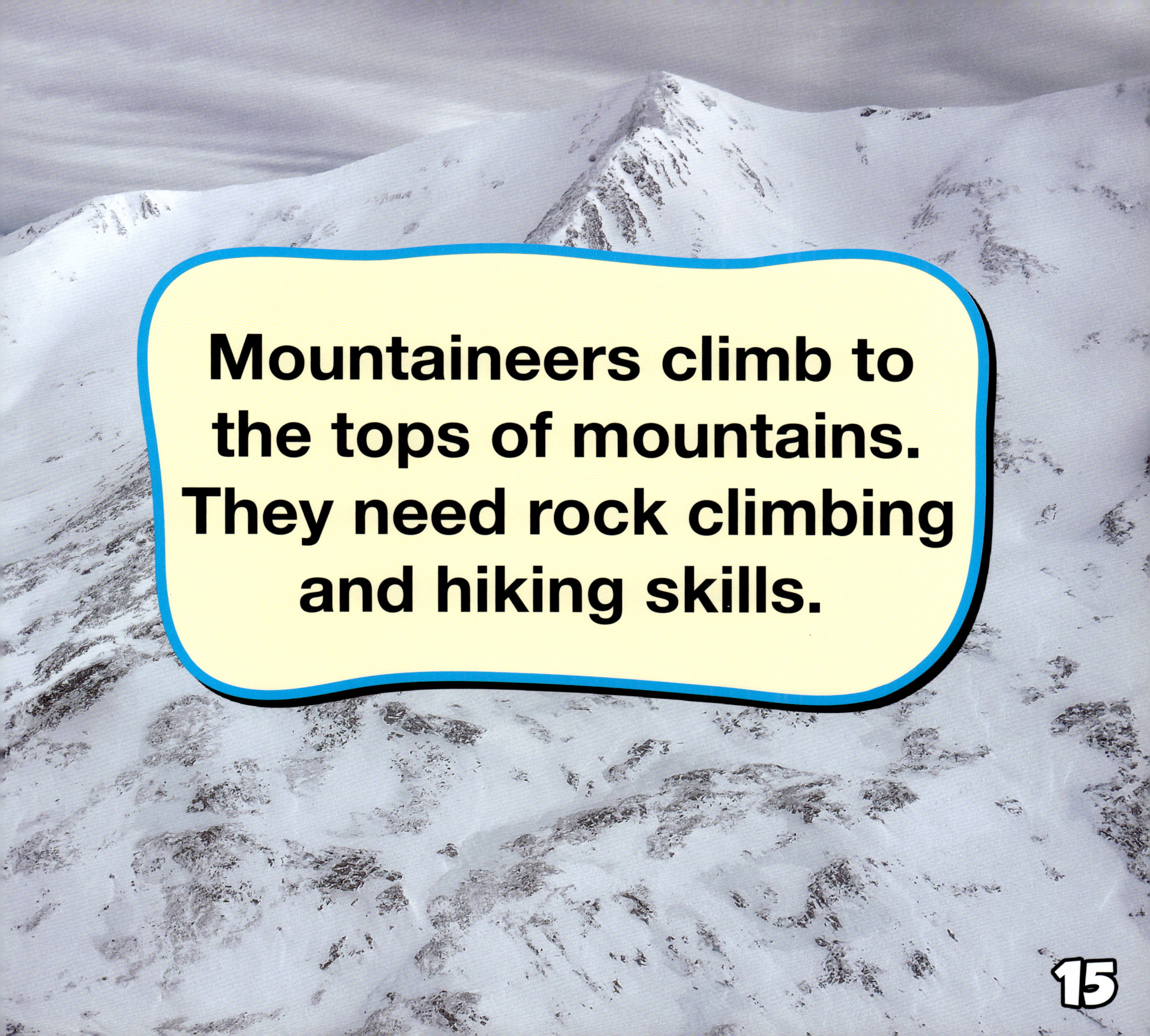

Mountaineers climb to the tops of mountains. They need rock climbing and hiking skills.

Whitewater kayakers use small, narrow boats. They travel down rivers with fast, rough water.

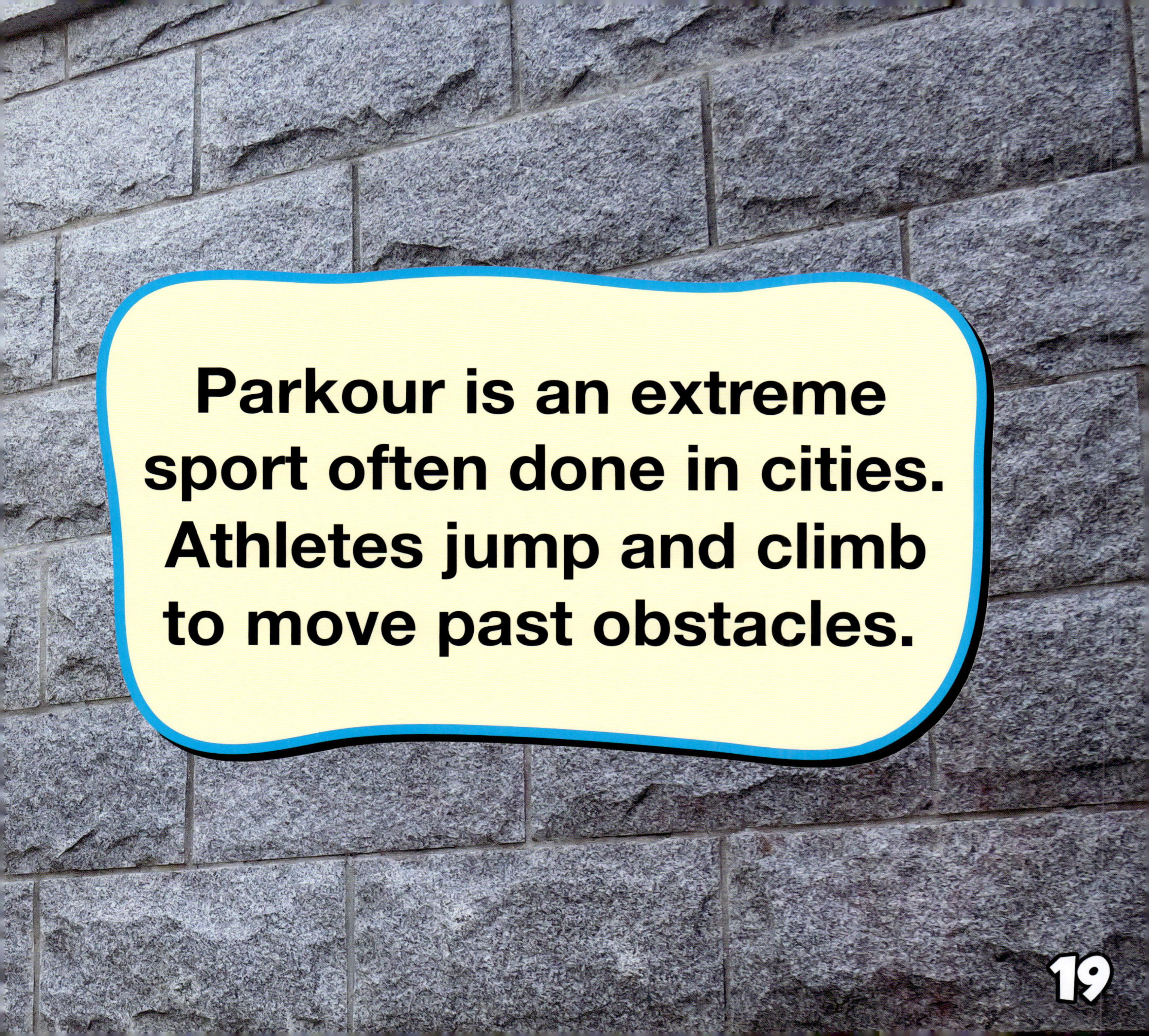

Parkour is an extreme sport often done in cities. Athletes jump and climb to move past obstacles.

Extreme sports can be very dangerous. It is important for athletes to learn to do their sport safely.

The **New River Gorge Bridge**, in West Virginia, is **open to BASE jumpers** for **one day** each year.

The **HIGHEST skydive** in history started at a height of **135,890 FEET** (41,419 meters).

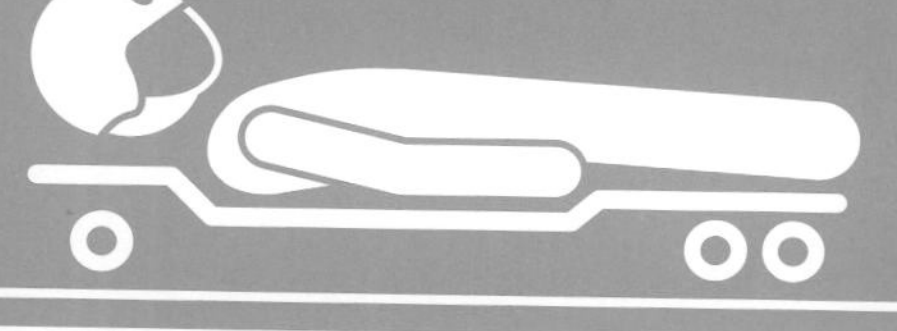

The **FIRST PROFESSIONAL street luge race** was held in California in **1975**.

People **first reached the top** of Earth's **highest mountain, Mount Everest,** in **1953**.

The **FIRST COUNTRY** to officially recognize **parkour as a sport** was Great Britain, in **2017**.

KEY WORDS

Research has shown that as much as 65 percent of all written material published in English is made up of 300 words. These 300 words cannot be taught using pictures or learned by sounding them out. They must be recognized by sight. This book contains 40 common sight words to help young readers improve their reading fluency and comprehension. This book also teaches young readers several important content words, such as proper nouns. These words are paired with pictures to aid in learning and improve understanding.

Page	Sight Words First Appearance
4	are, for, need, often, these, to, use, very
7	a, from, high, places, stops, the, them, they
8	and, land, their
11	is, most, of, one
12	at, down, on
15	mountains
16	rivers, small, water, with
19	an, in, move
20	be, can, do, important, it, learn

Page	Content Words First Appearance
4	athletes, extreme sports, tools
7	bungee jumpers, cord, ground
8	airplanes, parachutes, skydivers
11	BASE jumping
12	boards, riders, sleds, speeds
15	mountaineers, skills
16	boats, kayakers
19	cities, obstacles, parkour

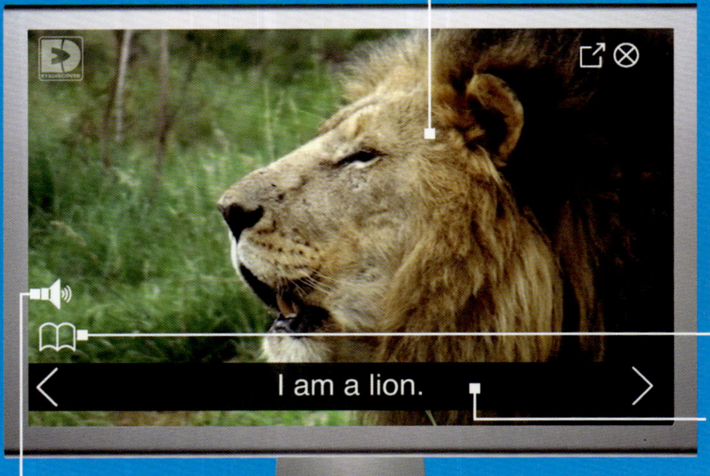

Watch
Video content brings each page to life.

Browse
Thumbnails make navigation simple.

Read
Follow along with text on the screen.

Listen
Hear each page read aloud.

Go to www.openlightbox.com and enter this book's unique code.

BOOK CODE

AVA43752